Pragmatic Team Dynamics:

Recognizing and Understanding the Forces at Work

By Lawrence G Fine

Pragmatic Team Dynamics: Recognizing and
Understanding the Forces at Work
Copyright © 2009 by (Kick It, LLC)

Table of Contents

Chapter 1: What is the 10-80-10 Rule?

A principle is the ultimate cause of something. It is a basic generalization accepted as a fundamental truth, a motivating force. Principles form the basis for reasoning and conduct.

The Pareto Principle

There is a popular principle in business referred to as the Pareto Principle. Its consistent application has improved productivity in businesses for years. Also known as the "80/20 Rule," this principle has proven effective over time in areas beyond the business arena. Simply stated, the 80/20 Rule means that in nearly all cases a few (20%) are vital to achieving a group's desired outcome, while others (80%) make more of a trivial contribution to the outcome. For example, 80% of the decisions in a meeting come from 20% of the time spent in the meeting. And we know that 80% of a manager's headaches come from the same 20% of the people being managed. It's been shown that 80% of customer complaints are caused by 20% of a company's product or services. Application of this principle to whatever data is being analyzed can generate valuable information that helps managers make better decisions. In management terms, it is very valuable in that it allows the manager to focus on the vital few (20%) rather than the trivial many (80%). Effort then can be focused where it will have the most impact.

The 10/80/10 Rule

After years of coaching many teams, I am convinced that there exists a similar, but slightly altered version, of the 80/20 Rule – the 10/80/10 Rule. This principle applies to sports teams, business teams, educational groups, and others. Every group has a designated leader who bears the responsibility for team success. This coach, organization president, or business team leader has a big job. As the leader, you carry many expectations, the largest one being that you will shape your team into a productive, winning, successful group. What's been overlooked, however, is that inside your group exists other unspoken leaders who may be competing with you or standing in the way of achieving your desired outcome.

Inside leaders – who are they? I call them the "10% positive leaders" and the "10% negative leaders." They comprise the top and bottom 10% of your team. The influence exerted by these leaders, as well as yourself, has tremendous effect on the other 80% of the group following their lead. Unless you are aware of them and working with these leaders, your team will never become all it was intended to be. Just as the Pareto Principle helps business leaders focus on the vital few in their group, the 10-80-10 Rule can help identify and manage the positive and negative leaders in a group. Much like the Pareto Principle helps a manager focus attention where it will have the most group impact, so will applying the 10-80-10 Rule to your group.

How do you identify the 10% positive leaders and 10% negative leaders? By paying attention to their leadership qualities and whether they are leading the remaining 80% closer to or farther away from the group's desired outcome. Once you know who is playing each role, you can guide them toward personal and professional success as well as the group's goal. Let's take a closer look at what these 10-80-10 group members are like.

10 % Positive Leaders

These leaders comprise the top 10% of the group. They effectively lead and influence members toward the group's common goal. Positive leaders have the team's best interest at heart and lead accordingly. They possess the personal and professional qualities needed to successfully lead a group. Befriending these leaders and helping them continue to develop and grow will help strengthen the group and move it toward that winning game, developing a new product or whatever the desired outcome may be. Much of the manager's focus should be spent on the personal development, training, and retention of these positive leaders.

The 80% Followers

The next 80 % of the people in your group have
willingly decided to follow the leader. These followers
have two choices: 1) effectively help the positive leaders
through support and hard work; or 2) take a more
ineffective, passive role in the group, leaning on the
leaders for support and direction. Effective followers
possess certain qualities that equip them to take an active
role in the group, while the ineffective followers possess a
different set of qualities.

Followers will follow both positive and negative
leaders in your group. The positive and negative leaders
are counting on their ability to persuade and are always
working to pull the followers toward their agenda. That
agenda is either working toward or away from the group's
goals. Tuning into who the followers are and helping them
develop strategies to protect themselves from the
influence of the negative leaders is invaluable in keeping
the team from sliding downhill. Also, looking for
followers who possess the potential to lead and become

leaders is the key to building team strength.

The Negative 10% Leaders

The remaining 10 % of your group members have often been referred to as the "trouble makers" or the "difficult" people. I suggest these group members be renamed to "**Negative Leaders.**" Leader, you say? Yes, a **Leader**. These members are influential, they get attention, they produce outcomes, they are in charge of money-making decisions, and are motivated by pay-offs. Sounds like a leader, doesn't it?

Why pay attention to these negative leaders? Manager need to because they cost the manager and the team in terms of time, money, and energy. They are also usurping the manager's power. A tremendous amount of energy will be spent dealing with negative leaders that could be much better spent on working with or rewarding the positive leaders and followers.

Group leaders sometimes have a tendency to overlook or ignore dealing with negative leaders. Perhaps they are not aware of them or they don't realize the dangerous impact the negative leaders imperceptibly cause or they simply don't know what to do with them so they leave them alone. Heed this wake-up call to recognize the power the negative leaders in a group can and will exert. Don't forget: these negative leaders are vying for the 80% followers as well as for the influence that positive leaders can have. It cannot be overstated or overstressed how much damage negative leaders can overtly or covertly do to a team.

Determining Who's Who

I truly believe a coach/teacher/CEO job includes working with people to make them better people as well as imparting their knowledge and love of the game, product being produced, or whatever your desired outcome is. You owe it to your team members to produce double dividends in their personal and professional lives.

I also believe that applying the 10-80-10 Rule makes this a possibility. Being able to determine who's who in your group not only grows group synergism, it also strengthens the group's identity and purpose. The biggest benefit to determining who in the group is most closely aligned with the 10-80-10 groupings can begin by determining where a person/player currently is: the top positive 10%, the 80% followers, or the 10% negative leaders.

First, make a plan to reproduce yourself from one or more of the positive leaders. Every leader should always be in the process of training someone to take his/her place. Second, try to separate the middle 80% from the bottom 10% so they can't be led astray. Third, try to lead the middle 80% in a positive direction. Finally, try to influence the negative leaders and see if there is a way to help some of them join the middle 80% or, ideally, become a part of the top 10% positive leaders. I believe a truly exceptional, outstanding coach/boss is able to convert their original 10-80-10 group ratio to one of 15-85-0 if they work long and hard enough with their team. I would also consider it a tremendous success just to move one or two people in the group to a new group. Let's begin your 10-80-10 journey by learning about what makes a positive leader.

Chapter 2: 10% Positive Leadership

The Chicago Bulls were in the finals against the Utah Jazz. They were down by a point with only seconds to go. Michael Jordan had the ball and everyone knew that he was going to take the final shot. Most of the defenders were around him. Instead of forcing the shot, he passed the ball to Steve Kerr, who made a three-point basket to win the game. Now that's leadership.

Bookshelves are filled with books offering answers to "what is leadership?" Leadership is a much-discussed phenomenon, but perhaps still one of the least understood. Therefore it's not surprising that the word leadership carries different definitions depending on whom you ask to define it. People have been trying to define it since the beginning of time.

Searching for a Definition

Definitions do exist and certain images and ideas seem to surface when trying to describe leaders. Keep in mind that most existing definitions and ideas on leadership have been developed and validated with white American males leading white American male followers. Certain ideas have seemed to stand the test of time and culture. Famous people have offered their definitions of what leadership is all about.

All of the great leaders have had one characteristic in common: it was the willingness to confront unequivocally the major anxiety of their people in their time. This, and not much else, is the essence of leadership – John K. Galbraith.

Great leaders are almost always great simplifiers, who can cut through argument, debate, and doubt to offer a solution everybody can understand. Leadership is the art of accomplishing more than the science of management says is possible – Colin Powell

Leadership is the potent combination of strategy and character. But if you must be without one, be without strategy – General H. Norman Schwarzkopf Jr.

Leadership is about having followers, those who willingly work their hearts out to get great work done. –
Unknown

There seems to be some general agreement that leadership is more of an art than a science: art referring to the leader's people skills and science being the knowledge they possess to get the job done. Simply put, good leaders artfully get the team to do what they wants done while using their know-how about getting the job done.

Leadership often arises in response to a need. This makes it more difficult to define, as the situations that give rise to it vary from circumstance to circumstance, group to group, and from one time in history to another. This implies that leadership can even be situational and relational.

Hollywood, books, TV shows, and movies certainly have made their contributions to providing us with images and ideas associated with leaders. These leaders, often portrayed more like heroes, romanticize, glorify, and even deify certain men and women who have saved the day. Faced with these preconceived (perhaps even fabricated) portraits of leaders only create more confusion as we go in search of a definition.

In addition to looking for ways to define what leadership is, sometimes it's helpful to look at what it is not. Certain myths about leadership have existed for centuries. Let's look at some common myths surrounding leadership.

Common Leadership Myths

A myth is a traditional story accepted as history. It serves to explain the world view of a particular people. It is a strong belief regarding some fact or phenomenon of experience. Ancients knew the power of myths and so do we today.

Myth: Leaders are born. They are not made.

Many people still think leaders are born and not made. Most people, however, have the potential of becoming a good leader. Many of our greatest leaders learned from watching others. Certain learned characteristics can make almost anyone a successful leader. Leadership is not an ability given only to a rare few – it is a set of learned skills and behaviors.

Myth: A woman does not make as good of a leader as a man.

It's no secret that men and women are different and do things in different ways. It's no secret that men and women are socialized differently throughout their life. Leadership is about leading people and women are generally more socialized to pay attention to people's needs and to know how to nurture people in the process while their needs are being met. While men and women may lead in different ways, a good leader is a good leader regardless of gender. There are female Fortune 500 leaders, NWBA captains, popular political figures, and many other leadership roles being successfully held by women.

Myth: Every leader must have charisma.

Charisma is that special, graceful, magical appeal that some people seem to possess that draws others to them. While many leaders are charismatic, most leaders are not. Some charismatic leaders take advantage of people's problems and offer them what seems to be a great solution. Charismatic leaders typically want their followers to be very dependent on them, which is the opposite of what good leaders want from those they lead. Not every charismatic leader has detrimental results (such as Jim Jones or Jim Bakker), but followers would be wise to beware of charismatic leaders. It's more helpful for leaders to think that their cause, purpose, and genuine, passionate desire to lead that make them charismatic, not the other way around.

Myth: The person assigned the title is the designated leader.

True leaders will rise to the top and others will naturally gravitate toward those they respect and want to work with. Therefore, true leadership is not based on a title or position – it is based on skills, abilities, performance, effectiveness, and passion. For example, the football coach may not have as much influence on his team as a player who can read the game and energize his teammates to victory. Or consider Gandhi, who through much of his life held no relevant, formal position.

Myth: The best leaders are the highly educated ones.

Many great leaders had little or no formal education. These leaders learned from watching other leaders and from their own experience. While knowledge of the job is important, leadership remains more an art than a science. Consider the self-made men and women in business, politics, and many other professions.

Qualities of Positive Leaders

No group/team can rise above the quality of its leaders. To identify a group's positive leaders a manager must have a good understanding of who they are, how they make decisions, how they interrelate with others, and their level of passion for the job. Positive leaders know themselves well. They know their strengths and nurture them. They know their weaker qualities and they position people with the needed strengths close by.

Personal Qualities

Positive leaders are people of high integrity. Leaders must already possess any quality that they are going to expect their team members to have. This collection of positive qualities and characteristics desirous in a leader is just that – a collection. This list is not complete, and you will never meet a person who possesses all of these qualities. Hopefully, though they will provide you with more insight into what to look for in your group.

Qualities – Any of the features that make something

what it is; the degree of excellence possessed.

Character – A distinctive mark; a distinct trait, moral strength, reputation

- **Passion –** Something that is desired intensely; driving or overpowering feeling or emotion. The most notable quality in great leaders is the passion they have for their people and their work. These leaders love what they do and love the members of their teams. This kind of passion inspires others to wholeheartedly join them and give their work a sense of purpose.

Life is action and passion therefore, it is required of a man that he should share the passion and action of the time, at peril of being judged not to live. – Oliver Wendell Holmes

- **Self-confidence -** Confidence in one's own abilities, belief in yourself and your own abilities. Positive leaders know who they are, what they need, and what they stand for. The leader's level of self-confidence will trickle down to the team members.

If I have lost confidence in myself, I have the universe against me. – Ralph Waldo Emerson

- **Visionary** - Being able to create new ideas and make plans on how to use them in ways that create a bright future. Having a clear sense of vision is important as well as the ability to articulate it to others. Taking the lead in shaping a future direction.

Vision - the art of seeing things invisible. - Jonathan Swift

- **High Energy** - Vigorous, dynamic, high-powered. Positive leaders tend to have boundless energy. They have learned to take care of themselves (physically, mentally, spiritually, and emotionally) and periodically take the time to re-energize themselves.

Energy and persistence alter all things. – Ben Franklin

- **Level-headed** - Exercising or showing good judgment; self-composed and sensible. Level-headed leaders make realistic leaders who know how to respond to problems and not just simply react or overreact to them. Leaders need to stay cool under pressure, which will inspire their followers to do the same. Remember, the knee-jerk is just that, a knee movement from a jerk – so don't do it, do not simply react.

Never give in, never, never, never, never, in nothing great or small, large or petty. Never give in except to convictions of honour and good sense. – Winston Churchill

- **Positive Attitude** - A positive state of mind and mood; how someone feels or thinks about something. Attitudes have a power all their own. Once they are set in motion they keep going and are hard to stop.

Leaders need to be optimists. Their vision is beyond the present. – Rudy Giuliani

- **Courage** - The willingness to take risks and accept responsibility for the outcome. A group will be no more courageous than the leader leading it. Leaders are often called upon to take courageous actions, such as staying optimistic in the face of problems, making tough decisions, confronting conflict, and standing firm when others disagree with them.

Knowledge is the antidote to fear. – Ralph Waldo Emerson

- **Honesty** - Integrity; sincerity, truthfulness. Positive leaders are always honest with those they lead. Working from a foundation of honesty builds trust in those who follow. Without an honest approach to leading, the leader will develop credibility problems.

I have found no greater satisfaction than achieving success through honest dealing and strict adherence to the view that, for you to gain, those you deal with should gain as well. – Alan Greenspan

- **Values** - Principles, standards considered worthwhile or desirable, esteemed principles. These guiding principles state how everyone who works in the group will conduct their business and behaviors. They become the foundation for the corporate or team culture; However, values can change over time in response to changing life experience.

I think if you look at people, whether in business or government, who haven't had any moral compass, who've just changed to say whatever they thought the popular thing was, in the end they're losers. – Michael Bloomberg

- **Determination** - Making or arriving at a decision; firmness of purpose; fixed intention or resolution. Just look at Michael Jordan! He didn't even make his high school basketball team.

Keep your dreams alive. Understand to achieve anything requires faith and belief in yourself, vision, hard work, determination, and dedication. Remember all things are possible for those who believe. - Gail Devers

- **Decisive** - Having the power to decide; conclusive, beyond doubt. In 1987, Bernie Marcus and Arthur Blank were fired from Handy Dan's, a home improvement store. They then decided to open their own business and now we have Home Depot. During crisis or critical times, leaders need to make good decisions. Positive, secure leaders will grant appropriate decision-making authority to others.

Making good decisions is a crucial skill at every level. – Peter Drucker

- **Open-minded** - Having or showing receptiveness to new and different ideas; curiosity, imperceptibility. Remaining open creates space for exploring all avenues when finding the best approaches or solutions. Positive leaders entertain all ideas and possibilities.

Without an open-minded mind, you can never be a great success. – Martha Stewart

- **Opportunity seeking** - Looking for favorable or

advantageous circumstances or combination of circumstances. Leaders are always looking for opportunities and for ways to convert those opportunities into something good. They are always looking forward for ways to continue building a successful company/team.

I'm not a sponge exactly, but I find that something I look at is a great opportunity for ideas. – Martha Stewart

- **Risk-Taker -** One who is willing to explore a course involving uncertain danger; ability to use good judgment, weighing the variability of returns from an investment. Positive leaders show a willingness to take calculated risks. Good leaders remain flexible and adaptable. They are also ready to take immediate action when needed as well as take responsibility for the consequences of their actions.

Uncertainty and expectation are the joys of life. – William Congreve

- **Goal Setter** - One able to determine the purpose toward which an endeavor is directed. Positive leaders influence the goals that are set and are responsible for creating the paths available to reach them. For goals to be understood and implemented, leaders should make them meaningful and measurable.

My philosophy of life is that if we make up our mind what we are going to make of our lives, then work hard toward that goal, we never lose - somehow we win out. - Ronald Reagan

- **Strong beliefs** - Something strongly believed in or accepted as the truth; especially a particular tenet adopted by a group of people. Leaders hold fast to their strong beliefs during whatever endeavor. Where others might bend or break their beliefs, leaders are steadfast.

I shall do less whenever I shall believe what I am doing hurts the cause and I shall do more whenever I shall believe doing more will help the cause. I shall try to correct errors when shown to be errors and I shall adopt

24

new views so fast as they shall appear to be true views. –
Abraham Lincoln

- **Discipline -** Training expected to produce a specific character or pattern of behavior. Discipline means daily practice and work. Sam Walton (WalMart) and John Geisse (Target) have spent the last 40 years making these two discount stores continually successful.

How am I going to live today in order to create the tomorrow I'm committed to? – Anthony Robbins.

- **Trustworthy -** Reliable; warranting trust; worthy of confidence; taking responsibility for one's actions. Positive leaders strive to be honest in all their dealing and the outcome of that is trust from those they lead.

Trust men and they will be true to you; treat them greatly and they will show themselves great. – Ralph Waldo Emerson

- **Emotional stability -** Possess the ability to be

stirred by emotions and yet remaining firm from change or variation; able to bounce back from change. A leader who can constantly stay cool under pressure inspires confidence to all around.

Happiness is not a matter of intensity but of balance, order, rhythm and harmony. - Thomas Merton

- **Maturity** - Having grown into full development of one's mental and physical and spiritual capacities. Mature leaders can set an example in that they can suffer disappointments gracefully. They are also comfortable with giving credit where credit is due. Maturity is kind of the old-fashioned word for what we now call emotional intelligence.

The three great essentials to achieve anything worthwhile are first, hard work, second, stick-to-itiveness, and third, common sense. – Thomas Edison

- **To empower** – To give power or authority to: sharing with others the power to do the job. Group members whose ideas are being implemented enhances their commitment to success. Positive leaders encourage self-development and high levels of job satisfaction with those they lead.

Outstanding leaders go out of their way to boost the self-esteem of their personnel. If people believe in themselves, it's amazing what they can accomplish. – Sam Walton

- **To motivate** – To stimulate people to exert more effort, energy, and enthusiasm in whatever they are doing. Positive leaders create a climate in which self-motivation prevails. They have a strong interest in the personal and professional development of those they lead. They encourage their team to give their personal bests. The focus of motivation is on action. Do not assume what motivates one team member to motivate another. Good leaders identify how each person on their teams respond to being motivated.

The companies that create the most nourishing environments for personal growth will attract the most talented people. – John Naisbitt

- **To be supportive** - Furnish support; providing assistance when needed. By providing support for their employees and customers by catering to their needs, Walgreens has become the nation's largest drugstore chain.

It is amazingly empowering to have the support of a strong, motivated, and inspirational group of people. - Susan Jeffers

- **To communicate clearly** - Exchanging thoughts, messages, or information by talking, writing, or behaviors. The danger for many who communicate is making sure the person who is being communicated to has received the message. We can sometimes assume too much in our communications.

Skill in the art of communication is crucial to a leader's success. He can accomplish nothing unless he can communicate effectively. – Norman Allen

An important aspect of managing our own development, as our relationships to others, is to authentically communicate our needs to others. Practice listening to what people do not say as well as what they do say. Two-way communication makes for good team relationships.

Basically our goal is to organize the world's information and to make it universally accessible and useful. – Larry Page

- **To nurture synergism** - To build a team with care. Building a team takes the ability to reach agreements among members of the team. Synergy is only created when leaders truly invest their time and efforts into fostering the success of everyone they are leading. Great leaders realize that their greatest resource is the people on their team. They are in tune with their followers.

The achievements of an organization are the result of the combined effort of each individual. – Vince Lombardi

- **Empathy** - The ability to share in another's emotions and feelings. Empathy skills are those that involve paying attention to what other people are saying, what they need, and the kind of relationship they value having. It's having the ability to see things from another's point of view.

Some people think only intellect counts; knowing how to solve problems, knowing how to get by, knowing how to identify an advantage and seize it. But the functions of the intellect are insufficient without courage, love, compassion, and empathy. - Dean Koontz

- **Commitment -** A pledge or promise to do something. Committed leaders will eventually develop committed followers. Commitment is the leader's emotional investment toward goals being pursued. Committed, hard-working leaders establish a long-term commitment to the people they are leading and the company's mission.

The time is always right to do what is right. - Martin Luther King Jr.

- **Enthusiasm -** Something arousing interest and zeal. Genuine enthusiasm is contagious. The level of enthusiasm a group or team displays is directly proportional to the leader's level. People look to their leader for enthusiasm.

Enthusiasm is everything. It must be taut and vibrating like a guitar string - Pelé

- **Loyalty** - Faithful adherence to a person or cause. Making decisions that take into consideration the follower's needs build loyalty for toward the leader. No one follows someone who they don't trust to have their best interest at heart. Feelings of loyalty are earned by the leader's actions.

Leadership is a two-way street, loyalty up and loyalty down. Respect for one's superiors and care for one's crew. – Grace Murray Hopper

- **Inner strength** - Finding your inner voice; the ability to move forward with, or without others. Many CEOs have arrived at their new companies only to find them in financial messes and with upheavals in personnel. Some leaders have turned these major companies around in nine months to a year making tough decisions they believed were the best all things considered.

Strength does not come from physical capacity; it comes from an indomitable will. – Mahatma Gandhi

WARNING: While these attributes are credited to positive leaders, negative leaders maybe equally skilled in some of them. They may be these skills to their own advantage and for their own agenda instead of what the group is trying to accomplish!

Leading from the Heart/EQ

Assuming a leadership position in today's workplace often requires an individual to demonstrate a high level of cognitive ability in order to process the complexity of information leaders face daily. Cognitive ability, of course, is our ability to "think" about things. Accessing things and processing them with a logical mind indicates a high IQ. Because so many incredibly bright CEOs/coaches were running into problems that eventually took their teams under, some researchers began to wonder if there was more to corporate success than just having a high IQ. And they found an answer.

In addition to having the high IQ and technical know-how to get the job done, they discovered that truly successful leaders had "the know-how" to work with people. The amount of people skills leaders possess has become known as their emotional intelligence or EQ. As one of the leading experts in the area of EQ, Daniel Goleman says, "It's a different way of being smart." Or as the Little Prince said, "It is the heart that sees rightly; what is essential is invisible to the eye." Learning to evaluate your leaders in terms of their EQ will give you another edge in building the team you desire.

What is Emotional Intelligence?

Since the 1980s and accelerating into the present there has become a growing interest in people's emotional intelligence. One of the first researchers to explore this idea in 1988 was Bar-On. He was the one that actually coined the term "Emotional Quotient." He described it as an array of traits and abilities related to a person's emotional and social knowledge that influences their overall ability to be successful. His model stressed the ideas that a high EQ consisted of:

1. The ability to be aware of, to understand, and to express oneself

2. The ability to be aware of, to understand and relate to others

3. The ability to deal with strong emotions and control one's impulses

4. The ability to adapt, to change, and to solve problems of a personal or social nature.

In 1997 Mayer and Salovey developed their model of emotional intelligence. They defined the concept more specifically as a person's ability to perceive emotions, to access them, and to generate emotions to assist thought to understand emotions and emotional knowledge and to reflectively regulate emotions to promote emotional and intellectual growth.

A more recent addition to thoughts on EQ is that of Goleman in 1998 in his book <u>Working with Emotional Intelligence</u>. Goleman defines EQ as how an individual's potential for mastering the skills of self-awareness, self-management, social awareness, and relationship management is worked out in practice. He states that these domains then become the foundation for learned abilities, what he calls "competencies." The EQ domain of self-awareness, for example, provides the underlying basis for the learned competency of accurate self-assessment of strengths and limitations pertaining to a role such as leadership.

That such competencies can be learned is a critical distinction between Goleman's idea and others. He believes the emotional competencies represent the degree to which an individual has mastered specific skills and abilities that build on the EQ and allow them greater effectiveness in the workplace. While other theories on EQ had a more generalized intent, Goleman specifically applies his ideas to the workplace. His competency-based approach reflects a tradition that emphasizes the identification of competencies that can be used to predict work performance over a variety of organizational settings, often with an emphasis on those in leadership positions.

Where does your EQ come from?

Our brain actually has two memories, one that stores and deals with ordinary facts and one that deals with emotionally charged ones. We all have many emotional lessons from childhood that have been stored in our subconscious. You can think of these as your emotional blueprints that you use to respond to situations. Our emotional lessons are shaped by our experiences throughout childhood. Of course, we also learn numerous facts from school and home. There is a continual two-way exchange between these two parts of our brain. While the emotional side is busy guiding our moment-to-moment decisions, it is also working closely with the rational mind, which is taking in its facts and trying to merge these two together. We can describe these two kinds of processes as intelligence and emotional intelligence. The ultimate goal is to harmonize the head and heart in all decisions you make. Our EQ is able to motivate oneself, persist in the face of frustration, regulate moods, and keeps distress from swamping our ability to think, to empathize, to hope.

Goleman defines emotional intelligence as this:

1. **Self-Awareness**: Knowing your emotions and being able to recognize your feelings as they are happening. Being able to monitor your feelings from moment to moment is crucial to bring you insight and understanding. It's being aware of both your mood and your thoughts about that mood. It's a non-judgmental, non-reactive attention to your inner state of being.

2. **Self-Regulation**. Managing your emotions vs. being a slave to them: Learning to handle feelings so they are appropriate to the situation builds your self-awareness. This gives you the capacity to soothe yourself and shake off the consequences of failure.

3. **Motivating Yourself** - Motivating your emotions

that guide you in reaching your goals is essential for reaching your goals. For self-motivation, and creativity emotional self-control, delay gratification.

4. **Having Empathy** – Having an awareness of other people's feelings and needs is what empathy is all about. The more open you are to your own emotions, the more skilled you become in reading other's feelings. Being able to hear the feelings behind what is being said is empathetic listening.

5. **Your Social Skills**. Developing skills (such as good listening, resolving conflict, negotiating, and nurturing) to work with others is vitally important. Leadership is not an issue of dominating your team members – instead, it is helping them work together to achieve a common goal.

As with developing intelligence, family life is your first school for emotional learning. It is here we learn how we feel about ourselves and how others react to our feelings. We learn how to think about these feelings and what choices we have in reacting – how to read and express hopes and fears.

Cultural Diversity

Never before has the fabric of our workplaces, classrooms, and communities been so global and culturally diverse. This diversity of followers makes the leader-follower relationship all the more complex. Leaders must be culturally competent.

What is Diversity?

In a general sense diversity, or multiculturalism, means recognizing the legitimacy of differences in people. More specifically, diversity includes a number of important human characteristics that affect an individual's value and opportunities and perceptions of self and others in the group. The main characteristics include age, ethnicity, gender, ability, race and sexual orientation. They also can include geographic location, military experience, work experience, religion, language, communication style, family status, work style and education.

Leaders' Challenge

The biggest challenge to leaders is how to interact productively despite the hurdles that cultural differences pose. This requires recognizing people as a product of their culture. People from different cultures may have different world views and values, different ways of talking, thinking, and dressing, and different ideas on their role of being a member of a group. Most importantly people from different cultures have differing perspectives on their definition and expectations of a leader. Not understanding these different perspectives can be stressful, confusing, and lead to conflict for everyone involved.

Positive leaders will become cultural learners. They will make an effort to understand each follower as an individual and get to know them as well as they can. They will find sources of encouragement for everyone around them. They will foster an attitude of tolerance as well as move beyond it to embrace and celebrate the rich dimensions of each individual.

Negative leaders will not leverage all of these

aspects of multicultural potential. Their focus will remain more on what needs to get done and will not make accommodations for the various ways in which people get things done. They will most likely perceive cultural differences as something to be endured as opposed to enjoyed.

10-80-10 Application

Hopefully you've now gained more insight into the top 10% of your group, your positive leaders. Though many definitions for leadership are available, they all seem to have some common core concepts, such as: Leaders are not necessarily born, but made by learning the appropriate skills and behaviors. Leaders bring different personal and professional strengths and weaknesses to your group. These strengths and weaknesses lie in the character and qualities of each leader. No one leader will possess them all, but some will possess more than others. The good news, again, is that people can also grow and acquire these qualities.

Leaders each haves their own level of IQ, their IQ

being their cognitive, critical thinking skills. A high IQ and the ability to apply it to the job are a valuable trait of any leader. Equally, if not more important, is a leader's emotional intelligence, or EQ. Their ability to emotionally relate to the group will determine how successful they become. Ideal leaders will have both a high IQ and a high EQ.

Good leaders are cultural learners trying their best to accommodate individual differences the team members will have.

While positive leaders are in demand, a leader is nothing without a group of followers to lead. Let's now turn our attention to the members of the group that comprise the largest number – the 80% followers.

Chapter 3: The 80 % Followers

In contrast to the bookshelves filled with writing on leadership, the shelves are rather empty when looking for a book on what it means to be an effective follower. That could be an indication of the value we place on leadership and or how we might undervalue followers. Whatever the reason, more insights into the role of followers would be welcome.

Followers and leaders develop a tight, reciprocal relationship where they influence one another as well as their organization or team. How vital it becomes then to know what comprises an effective and ineffective follower. Could it be just as important as understanding what makes a leader tick? Yes.

Searching for a Definition

Followers, like leaders, come in all shapes, sizes,

gender, and personalities. Like leaders the vast majority of followers are made and hence can learn how to become effective followers. The term "follower," like "work leader," conjures up images in our minds. These images and ideas have developed over time. Certain ones have stood the test of time. Others are always being reshaped by the minds that enjoy being an effective follower. What comes to your mind when you hear the word "follower?" Here are some definitions from the experts:

Followers are people of exceptional ability who know how to lead themselves. The people who actually contribute more than 80% of any organization. Robert Kelly, Author of The Power of Followership

Followership is the real people factor in the other 80-90% that makes for great success. – Walter Kiechel, Fortune

Followership is the individual desire to serve others and support a team in its task to complete a mission. Followers seek to perform their tasks well, maintain cooperative working relationships, provide constructive disagreement, share leadership functions and support leadership development. – Leading Today magazine.

For estimating the intelligence of a ruler, look at the men he has around him. – Machiavelli, The Prince.

Leaders rarely use their power wisely or effectively over long periods unless they are supported by followers who have the stature to help them. – Ira Chaleff, The Courageous Follower.

The recurring theme in these quotes is that effective followers are critical to a leader's success. Followers are described with many names, including co-workers, associates, teammates, students, disciples, colleagues, and so on. No matter the name, effective followers follow their leader and form a reciprocal partnership.

Followers, unlike leaders, are more times than not the unsung heroes and heroines. That does not translate into leaders being the only ones with power or a list of personal achievements. As the supporting cast, followers generally do not receive the fame or huge salaries that leaders do. You won't see many movies called the "Portrait of a Follower." Followers have tremendous responsibilities and receive little glory, but let's face it: without willing followers, there would be no leaders. No coach, CEO, president, or any other leader would accomplish much without their followers.

Common Followership Myths

As with leadership, certain stereotypes and myths surround the definition of a follower. Remember, a myth is traditional story accepted as history. It serves to explain the world view of a particular people. It is a strong belief regarding some phenomenon or experience. Myths are hard to reshape or let go of and therefore have a strong hold on many people.

Myth: Followers should mindlessly follow their leader

Followers have every right to stop following their leader when it's appropriate to protect themselves. High quality followers follow with intelligence, enthusiasm, and their own moral strength. Blind obedience is what leads to mindless following. Quality followers keep a close eye on their leaders. They never stop thinking for themselves or relinquish any decision-making power when they feel like it is wrong or inappropriate.

The traditional notion that leaders are active and followers are passive is a misconception. Followers can and need to challenge their leaders when necessary. Effective followers do not remain silent, which can be interpreted as consent of a leader's actions.

Myth: Followers never become leaders

At West Point and other military schools, leadership is a reward for good followership. How many times do great military and political leaders get moved up the ranks because of their impeccable ability to follow those in charge? In business this process is more often is referred to as climbing the ladder. Some refer to it as an on-going loop – leaders create followers, who create leaders. Good leaders are always in the process of recreating themselves in someone else.

Myth: It's easier to follow than lead.

Effective following is not about sitting back and enjoying the ride. It's a powerful position. Followers help to define and shape the leader who is leading as well as the mission of the organization. Recall Kiechel's quote that says followers do 80% of the work that leads to great success. Followers can exert the same creativity, intelligence, and other talents with zeal equal to the leader's.

Myth: People have no choice in whom they follow.

Following is a choice: an active, essential choice. Followers have a choice to support who or what they want. Followers must willingly submit themselves to team, business, classroom, and all other organizations. Followers must stay on their guard so they can stop following any leader who crosses their ethical, moral, or any other value they hold dear.

Leader & Follower Relationship

Followers define and shape the leader's actions. They affect the strength of the leader's influence, dictate the style by which the leader leads, and ultimately decide whether the group reaches its goals or not. You don't want to leave your group's leader-follower relationship to chance. It's vital to understand this reciprocal relationship.

- Leaders and followers both are vital to achieving the group's desired outcome.
- Without a common goal and willing followers, there are no leaders.
- Followers and leaders develop a relationship where they influence one another as well as the organization, team, or any group.
- Leadership only exists in the perception of the followers.
- Followers, like leaders, know and understand themselves and what they want.
- You can't have effective leaders without responsive followers.

- Followership is the flip side of leadership.

Types of Followers

Just as there are different kinds of leaders, there are different kinds of followers. Experts have developed different descriptions of the roles followers can play:

In their article "Followership, Followers, and Following," Fyodor Dostoevsky and Paul Di Carlo offer a 5-P Model where they categorize followers as:

- **Participants:** Those actively involved and contributing to moving forward;
- **Pessimists:** Those who think that change means we are doomed and need to share this with everyone;
- **Passengers:** Those who are only there in body while their mind is elsewhere;
- **Pigs:** Those only there for the food
- **Prisoners:** Those who are present, but not by their choice.

Effective followers resemble the participants, while the ineffective followers possess the pessimistic, passenger, pig, and prisoner roles. You can use these colorful P's when observing the habits of your team members.

Robert Kelly, in his article, "In Praise of Followers" describes five fellowship patterns:

- **Sheep:** As he calls them, are passive and uncritical. These followers lack initiative and a sense of responsibility. They perform the required task and then stop.
- **Yes People:** These followers appear to be livelier but are equally unenterprising like the sheep. They depend on the leader for inspiration and can be aggressively deferential. Some leaders like them and can even form alliances with them that can stifle their creativity and energy.
- **Alienated Followers:** These are critical and independent thinkers but take a passive role. They are cynical but perform with a disgruntled attitude. They seldom actively oppose anything or speak

up.

- **Survivors:** These are the followers who go along with the leaders, usually because they believe it is better to be safe than sorry. They are adept at surviving change.

- **Effective Followers:** These followers perform with energy and assertiveness. They are critical, independent thinkers and will pro-actively challenge decisions. They are risk-takers and problem-solvers. They can usually work without strong leadership.

Personal Qualities of Effective and Ineffective Followers

Just as leadership requires some special qualities, so does followership. Here are some desirable qualities, their definitions, and some quotes from various leaders in their own area. Again the list is an ideal collection of traits and no one follower is going to possess them all. Hopefully, though, they can get you better acquainted with the qualities of the effective and ineffective followers on your team.

Quality - Any of the features that make something what it is; the degree of excellence possessed.

Character - A distinctive mark; a distinct trait, moral strength, reputation.

Effective Followers

- **Self-directed** - Directed or guided by oneself; free from external control and constraint. It's important for followers to maintain the desired partner dynamics with the leader. Leaders must be able to count on their followers to take an active role and be able to lead themselves to get things done.

The only limit to your impact is your imagination and commitment. – Anthony Robbins

- **Active** - Marked by energetic activity, being in a state of action. Followers must speak out about what's consistent and inconsistent with their personal and professional business goals.

Followers must become good perceivers of how the leader is performing.

I have nothing to offer but blood, toil, tears, and sweat. – Winston Churchill

- **Willing** - Inclined; prepared to act gladly. Followers exercise their free will, not coercion, when deciding on who will lead them. They willingly step forward to play the part of a successful team.

Work is the very fire where we are baked to perfection, and like the master of the fire itself, we add the essential ingredient and fulfillment when we walk into the flames ourselves. – David Whyte

- **Empowered** - To give power or authority to; sharing with others the power to do the job. Followers should expect leaders to care for them, respect them, treat them with dignity, and make efforts to meet their needs.

Power can be taken, but not given. The process of

the taking is empowerment. – Gloria Steinem

- **Assertive** - Willing to take charge; inclined toward bold and confident assertion; self-assured. It takes courage and skill to speak up, but it is vitally important to give leaders honest feedback. Assertiveness opens the door for a two-way conversation.

The basic difference between being assertive and being aggressive is how our words and behaviors affect the rights and well-being of others. – Sharon A. Bower

- **Ethical** - Being in accordance with the accepted right and wrongs that govern the conduct of a profession. Followers should never be put in a position by any leader to violate their ethics.

Try not to become a man of success, but rather try to become a man of value. – Albert Einstein

- **Loyalty** - Faithful adherence to a person or cause. Followers can give or withhold their loyalty to leaders. Leaders need to engage followers in mutual pursuits.

An ounce of loyalty is worth a pound of cleverness.
– Elbert G. Hubbard

- **Trustworthy** - Reliable; warranting trust; worthy
  of confidence; taking responsibility for one's
  actions. Followers who are open and honest about
  their responsibilities and how they are performing
  them will gain trust from the leader.

Trust is our trail guide through the wilderness of
change. – Bill McCarthy

- **Honest** - Integrity, sincerity; truthfulness.
  Followers should work to keep themselves and
  their leaders honest.

The purpose of competition is not to beat someone
down, but to bring out the best in every player. - Walter
Wheeler

- **Courage** - The willingness to take risks and accept
  responsibility for the outcome. It takes courage to

follow any leader. Courage is required to challenge a leader's thinking or action. It takes much more courage to be an active follower than a passive one.

We won't even attempt to achieve what we do not believe at a deep level we can have or deserve. – Fay B.

- **Supportive** - Furnish support; providing assistance when needed. Followers have a choice in terms of offering support. It helps to understand how the pressure on leaders can weigh them down and try to minimize the things that add pressure and bring out the leader's strengths for the good of the group. Two-way support is essential in the leader-follower relationship.

Light is the task when many share the toil. – Homer

- **Responsible** - To be required to give an account; personal accountability. Followers need to help the leader stay on track as well as be responsible for their part of the team's work.

The choice we offer people is what creates accountability. – Peter Block

- **High performance standard** - Degree or level of requirement; the act or style of performing a role at work to the best of your ability. Followers are continually learning, updating their skills, and seeking out extra work when necessary and appropriate.

My success just evolved from working hard at the business at hand each day. – Johnny Carson

- **Informed** - To make aware of something; to provide information. It's important for followers to know what's going in at all levels of work.

Real knowledge is to know the extent of one's ignorance. – Confucius

- **Encouraging** - To inspire with hope, courage or confidence; to spur on followers can encourage other followers as well as leaders with their encouragement. People love to be encouraged, regardless of the position they hold.

There are high spots in all of our lives and most of them have come about through encouragement of someone else. I don't care how successful or how famous a man or woman may be, each hungers for applause. – George M. Adams

- **Inner strength** - The will to keep on going when everyone else is flagging or failing. All of us get tired from time to time. The older we get, the more we find that we can't just keep going. That's when you need the inner resolve and toughness to keep going and get through to the completed task or project.

Strength does not come from physical capacity; it comes from an indomitable will. – Mahatma Gandhi

- **Positive attitude** - A positive state of mind and mood. How someone feels or thinks about something; attitudes have a way of gaining their own momentum, and once they begin to move in a particular direction are hard to stop.

You are not here merely to make a living. You are here to enable the world to live more amply, with greater vision, with a finer spirit of hope and achievement. You are here to enrich the world and you impoverish yourself when you forget the errand. – Woodrow Wilson

- **High self-esteem** - Pride in oneself; the quality of being worthy of esteem and respect. Followers need a high self-esteem to continue to think for themselves as they are being lead.

Companies that create the most nourishing environments for personal growth will attract the most talented people. – John Naisbitt

- **Fair** - Just to all parties; equitable leaders need to be able to engage their followers in mutual pursuits.

Men are born equal but they are also born different. – Erich Fromm

- **Empathetic** - The ability to share in another's emotions and feelings. Empathy skills are those that involve paying attention to what other people are saying, what they need, and the kind of relationship they value having. It's the ability to see things from another's point of view.

When we go outside of ourselves and focus on others' needs, we expend our energy in caring as opposed to acting out of fear. – Anonymous

Non-Effective Followers

Not all followers are effective. Some are coasters, there to meet minimal standards and make no effort to do more. Some merely join by adding their name to a membership list and are only there for résumé gain. The ineffective follower does what is asked and nothing more.

- **Passive** - Waiting for the information to be provided. Passive followers will move or change once they get the answers to their questions. Silence can be interpreted as support as well as lack of support.

It's always too early to quit. – Jason Kidd

61

- **Undisciplined** - Not subject to discipline or correction, the opposite of being willing to train.

  By constant self-discipline and self–control you can develop greatness of character. – Grenville Kleiser

- **Unmotivated** - Having no motivation or incentive; little desire to give their personal best; little or no interest in personal or professional development. Unmotivated followers may swing back and forth between positive and negative leaders.

  Motivation is what gets you started. Habit is what keeps you going. – Jim Ryun

- **Uninformed** - Not having, showing, or making use of information, not informed; closed to hearing new information. An uninformed follower is ignorant and often times a suspicious follower. Because they make little or no effort to find out what's going on, they are subject to being persuaded by rumors.

  There is only one good, knowledge, and one evil,

ignorance. – Socrates

- **Not a team player** - Focuses more time and energy on self-interest, as opposed to group interest; they are more inclined to pull team members away from the team goal than push them toward it. The may even create divisive relationships within the group.

Individual commitment to group effort – that is what makes a team work, a company work, a society work, a civilization work. – Vince Lombardi

- **Cynical** - Expressing jaded or scornful skepticism or negativity; pessimistic. Cynicism is often anger expressed in a humorous way directed toward the person who is making them angry.

Cynicism is the humor of hatred. – Sir Herbert Beerbohm Tree

- **Unethical** - Not conforming to approved standards of social or professional behavior. Unethical followers do not always play by the rules. They can often be persuaded to forgo their own sense of ethical behavior regarding a situation for the right pay-off.

The right to swing my fist ends where the beginning of the other man's nose begins. – Oliver Wendell Holmes

- **Negative attitude** - A negative state of mind or feeling; no matter what the situation is the person feels angry about it and develops a negative mindset. Negative attitudes have a momentum all their own, and once it gets started it is contagious and hard to stop.

Those who think the world is a dark place are blind to the light that might illuminate their lives. – Wayne Dyer

- **Uncaring** - Devoid of concern or feeling; lacking in affection or warm feelings. Uncaring followers tend to develop an apathetic outlook to other team members and the leader.

Caring is a powerful business advantage. – Scott Johnson

- **Critical** - Inclined to judge severely and find fault. Critical followers are also looking and ready to take advantage of finding fault with someone or something. They live to criticize and hurt others while somehow in the process feeling a little better about themselves.

It is much easier to be critical than it is to be correct. – Benjamin Disraeli

- **Unsupportive** - Not furnishing support or assistance. Unsupportive followers give little or no assistance to the team, its goals, or its leaders.

One man can be a crucial ingredient on a team, but one man cannot make a team. – Kareem Abdul-Jabbar

- **Impatient** - Unable to wait patiently; unable to endure irritation. Impatient followers want things done and done now. They complain about things not getting done or getting done fast enough.

Patience is not passive; on the contrary, it is active, it is concentrated strength. – Edward G. Bulwer-Lytton

- **Negative influence** - Negative, imperceptible power affecting people.

It is easier to influence strong than weak characters in life. – Margot Asquith

- **Irresponsible** - Marked by lack of responsibility. These followers may engage in taking inappropriate, uncalculated risks without asking other team members or the leader.

With power comes great responsibility. – Superman's Uncle

- **Critical** - Inclined to judge other severely and find fault. Criticalness is displayed in forms of disrespect and negativity toward others. Critical people often are intolerant of other's ideas, beliefs, and general sense of self.

The resentment that criticism engenders can demoralize employees, family members, and friends, and still not correct the situation that has been condemned. – Dale Carnegie

- **Dependent** - Contingent on another; relying on the aid of another for support.

No degree of knowledge attainable by man is able to set him above the want of hourly assistance. – Samuel Johnson

- **Rebellious** - Resisting treatment or control; unruly. Creating conflict or harm intentionally; resistant to the need to change. Rebellious followers will not conform to group rules or group plans.

What is a rebel? A man who says no. – Albert Camus

- **Aggressive** - Inclined to behave in an actively, openly hostile fashion; forcing ideas on others. Aggressive behavior tries to force others to think and act particular ways, perhaps even ways that are not appealing.

Remove severe restraint and what will become of virtue. – Seneca

- **Discouraging** - To deprive of hope, confidence and spirit.

Discouragement is the opposite of courage. – Connie Tilley

- **Disloyal** - Lacking loyalty; undermining the efforts of others.

Unless you can find some sense of loyalty you cannot find unity and peace in your active living. – Josiah Royce

10-80-10 Application

The interdependent leader-follower relationship is of utmost importance and should not be left to chance. Leaders and followers develop a dual relationship where they influence one another (positively or negatively) while trying to achieve the group's desired outcome.

Experts have described different types of followers. Followers who fit these descriptions either enhance the group they are a part of or detract from achieving the group's goals. Identifying what kind of followers you have in your group will help you to focus your attention where it is most needed. There are effective followers and ineffective followers who possess different personal and professional qualities. Again, being more aware of these qualities can help you identify areas your followers may need to grow in.

Remember that your 80% followers are sandwiched in between your 10% positive leaders and your 10% negative leaders. These leaders are constantly vying for your followers' attention. Your job becomes one of doing your best to separate the followers from the 10% negative leaders and helping the followers develop their own strategies to protect themselves from such a negative influence.

That leaves the 10% negative leaders to become more familiar with. These negative leaders can be as artful as the positive ones, making it difficult to easily see who they are. Who are these negative leaders? The next chapter has some answers.

Chapter 4: The 10 % Negative Leaders

Negative and positive leaders are at opposite ends of the power struggle - the top and bottom 10%. The negative influence from these leaders has been shown to have a direct correlation to the development of a business, team, classroom or any group. This correlation reveals that the more negative influence there is, the more the potential results of everyone in the group, and hence the group as a whole, goes down. Negative leaders have gained a reputation of destroying, not enhancing, the potential of the group. Although different groups may seek to accomplish different goals, ultimately the negative leaders, like the positive ones, realize that the mainstay of their job is to lead people. Negative leaders possess certain qualities and characteristics that tend to feed their negative outlook. These qualities and characteristics keep them from leading effectively and realizing their potential positive leadership ability. You must make every effort to identify your negative leaders and keep them from destroying your group.

Search for a Definition

The word negative, no doubt, brings certain images and ideas to mind. But what about the combination of words "negative leader?" What kinds of pictures and feelings are you experiencing now? Does "negative leader" sound like an oxymoron to you? Two words which are opposite and contradictory?

History, politics, sports, education, religion, and many other powerful areas of our lives have been and continue to be strongly influenced by negative leaders. Negative leaders' motivations and behaviors are different, yet may resemble those in leadership positions. Negative leaders, like positive ones, can be good at making decisions, have qualities that attract others to them, have goals in mind to achieve, have passion for their work, appear to have great self-confidence, are risk-takers, and enjoy the power that comes with being the leader. Just like positive leaders, they are passionate about achieving outcomes that appeal to themselves and the group they are serving. They generally have no second thoughts about abusing their power, misusing their power, or leading others in directions they will someday probably regret going in order to get the job done.

Sometimes positive leaders in a group will refer to these negative leaders as "difficult people" to deal with or "troublemakers" to keep an eye on. I strongly suggest giving these people the title they really deserve: "negative leader." Giving them an equally powerful title as the positive leaders may help remind you of the equal or greater power they hold in the group. Negative leaders are passionately competing with the positive leaders to gain an influence on the group as well as trying to strongly influence the 80% followers to follow them. Hence, you need to have a clear understanding of who these negative leaders are and how they are impacting your group.

Common Myths about Negative Leaders

Myths exist concerning the negative leader just like they do for the positive leaders and followers. Remember that myths are traditional stories or ideas that explain a person's world view Myths are hard to reshape or let go of. Because of this, they have a strong hold on people.

Myth: Negative leaders are easy to spot

Because they demonstrate leadership capabilities, negative leaders may not be easy to identify initially. Many negative leaders can be enigmas. This simply means that they are talented enough to baffle those in charge as they can play both sides against each other without the other knowing it. This confusing ability keeps group leaders off balance in terms of their ability to read these negative leaders.

Myth: Negative leaders do not attract others to them.

On the contrary, some negative leaders can be as charismatic, if not more than, positive leaders. Many negative leaders use their charisma to draw to them people who are looking for someone to depend on. These followers become so enthralled and so unhealthily attached to the leaders that they will do anything for them. Negative leaders' influences can be so strong that people will even commit tragic crimes for them, just like Hitler's followers did for him.

Myth: Negative leaders are never successful

Have you ever heard a coach barking instructions or screaming critical comments at players during a game? How about the Saturday morning park district league coach who constantly yells critical comments at the players, who are only third-graders. These coaches can be heard saying hurtful things that affect the kids' personally as well as their desire to pursue playing the game. Or how about the college coach who gets so mad he throws chairs out on the game floor or argues with the referees so violently he gets a technical called. And yet, when the final play is made, the teams of these less than desirable coaches have WON the game. Does the end justify the means at any level of the group's best interest? Does this really classify as a win for anyone?

Myth: Negative Leaders are Easy to Change

Changing someone's behavior is hard work even when they decide they want to commit to making change. Trying to change negative leaders who are happy being successful negative leaders is difficult. It's not that a negative leader can't learn new skills and behaviors and become a more positive leader. Of course, the million-dollar question becomes "What do you do with negative leaders that do not want to change?" How long and to what degree can you afford to keep them as part of your team? Conversely what will be the impact to the team if you remove them from the team and their followers also leave?

Qualities and Characteristics

Negative leaders, like positive leaders and followers, have certain qualities and characteristics that make them who they are. The following list of qualities is a collection, not an exhaustive list of characteristics possessed by negative leaders. No negative leaders will possess them all, but many possess many of them. A negative leader can be recognized by the following qualities and characteristics. Some of these qualities may not sound so desirable. All the more reason to believe and remember: Negative leaders are not desirable!

>**Qualities** - Any of the features that make something what it is; the degree of excellence possessed.

>**Characteristics** - A distinctive mark; a distinct trait; moral strength; reputation

- **Intimidating** - To make timid; to fill with fear; to coerce or inhibit by or as if by threats. This will only work for a relatively short period. Eventually

77

someone will stand up to the intimidation or will simply change jobs.

Some of us just go along ... until that marvelous day people stop intimidating us or should I say we refuse to let them intimidate us. – Peggy Lee

- **Blamer** - To hold responsible; to place responsibility for an outcome on someone else. There must be a balance between being held responsible for the work that we do and taking the blame for something that someone else in the team has failed to do properly. Take care of the balance and refuse to accept the blame when it is not yours.

I never blame myself when I'm not hitting. I just blame the bat and if it keeps up, I change bats. After all, I know it isn't my fault that I'm not hitting, how can I get mad at myself. – Peter Berra

- **Quitter** - Someone who gives up; putting aside or discontinuing. All too often employees run away from becoming responsible for something or someone. Even the subordinate can run away and cause problems for the entire team when their workload is added to everyone else's.

Many people give up just when they're about to achieve success. They quit on the one-yard line. They give up at the last minute of the game, one foot from a winning touchdown. – Ross Perot

- **Poor communicator** - To poorly convey information; struggle to make a sensible meaning. In Far Eastern countries to ask someone to explain what they mean is counter to cultural behavior. The communicator and the one hearing both lose face in such an encounter. We must be careful in our communications with people of other cultures that they clearly understand what we have to say. We cannot assume someone understands even if they are from a similar culture. For example people from Texas may assume one thing but people from New York may understand it totally differently.

The most important thing in communication is to

hear what isn't being said. – Peter Drucker

- **Close-minded** - Not open to new ideas or ways of doing things; intolerant of the beliefs and opinions of others; stubbornly unreceptive to new ideas. Business will always have an undercurrent of new ideas or new work practices. The attitude "we've always done it this way" will kill new ideas and actions. A closed mind will never make progress.

The leader must never close the gap between himself and the group. He must walk a tightrope between the consent he must win and the control he must exert. – Vince Lombardi

- **Pessimist** - Someone who tends to stress the negative; to take the gloomiest view possible. Is the glass half full or half empty? The real pessimist will say there is some water in the glass, but is not prepared to see it as half empty. It is hard to convince someone like that of any task that is difficult to do has the possibility of being completed.

When you live your life with an appreciation of coincidences and their meanings, you connect with the underlying field of infinite possibilities. - Deepak Chopra

- **Power seeker** - Someone who is always looking for the official capacity to exercise control over others. Having power over other people seems to be the motivation behind many supervisors or managers, but that desire does not make them effective at exercising that power.

It is said that power corrupts, but it's more true that power attracts the corruptible. The sane are usually attracted to something else. – David Brin

- **Arrogant** - Having or displaying a sense of over-bearing self-worth or self-importance; a feeling or assumption of one's superiority. All too often the arrogant will be tripped up by their own self-importance, but will not be prepared to learn from it. We all need to learn. If we pass a day or a week without learning something, we are in danger of falling into arrogance.

The most important scientific revolutions all include, as their only common feature, the dethronement of human arrogance from one pedestal after another of previous convictions about our centrality in the cosmos. – Stephen Jay Gould

- **Irrational risk taker** – Not having good reasons to take an uncalculated risk. Not exercising sound judgment. How do we judge good and bad risk? This is the question that is being asked by banks all over the world. Many of them made enormous sums of money taking risks, but those risks have now come back to haunt them. Some banks have disappeared, having been swallowed up by bigger banks. Others needed government bailouts to keep them in business.

We expect others to act rationally even though we are irrational. – Scott Adams

- **Self-serving** - Serving one's own interest without concern for the needs of others; sole concern for one's own interest. Managers need to be team players in terms of serving the needs of the company and not themselves. All too often we find individuals putting their interests first.

Life is not meaningful to us unless serving an end beyond itself, unless it is of value to someone else. – Abraham Herschel

- **Hasty** - Done or made too quickly to be accurate or wise. Sometimes we have to make snap decisions. There is a line from the film S.W.A.T. that talks about a policeman having to make an instant decision, and then his boss having weeks to review it and make a judgment. Sometimes time is of the essence, but we must make use of all available time to make an accurate analysis of the situation and when all is done we can make the final decisions in the required time-frame. Often it is not easy to balance someone else's time limits with your decision-making process.

Haste in every business brings failure. – Herodotus

- **Indecisive** - Characterized by indecision; not able

to clearly make a decision. Some people are made like this; others were not allowed to make even simple decisions while they were growing up and so in adulthood they become afraid of making decisions.

Using the power of decision gives you the capacity to get past any excuse to change any and every part of your life in an instant. – Anthony Robbins

- **Immature** - Not fully grown or developed; a lack of maturity. Some are late developers when it comes to maturity; others are still children at heart. We must all take the responsibility for ourselves, our families, and the business in which we work.

The mark of an immature man is that he wants to die nobly for a cause, while the mark of a mature man is he wants to live humbly for one. – J.D. Salinger

- **Aimless** - Devoid of direction or purpose. Those who aim at nothing get nothing. The aimless person will achieve little and allow everyone else to accomplish everything.

We must have a theme, a goal, a purpose in our lives. If you don't know where you're aiming, you don't have a goal. My goal is to live my life in such a way that when I die someone can say, she cared. – Mary Kay Ash

- **Short-sighted** - Lacking foresight or scope. The physical parallel of being short-sighted is a very visual example. When looking at a situation or a problem, the whole of the problem and its solution must be seen. A clear view of what must be done and and how to do it then must be developed. Sometimes this is not possible without project planning software. However, even using a software-based project management tool, all managers need to review the tasks to ensure completeness of the task list as well as completeness of the project as a whole. So a clear view of the problem, project or task in front of us is essential.

To go beyond is as wrong as to fall short. – Confucius

- **Unfair** - Not just; unethical; showing favoritism.

All of us have a capacity for favoritism. We all get along better with some people than others. It may be because of our ethnic background or the area of our country in which we live, or it may simply be that we share common interests and hobbies. The danger is when friendship and camaraderie becomes favoritism. We find that the favorites get the best jobs and promotions and those not in favor get a rough time. Actions like this spoil the team dynamics and destroy company loyalty.

It is not fair to ask of others what you are not willing to do yourself. – Eleanor Roosevelt

- **Uncaring** - Lacking concern or sympathy without thought or care for others. Everyone can hit a crisis. It may be planned, like the birth of a child, or unplanned, like the illness of an employee or a member of their close family. Most people face crises in their lives at some time or another. That is the time when they need to find they can "cut some slack" and look after their family and return to look after any tasks or projects at a later date. It helps the team when they know someone is hurting that they see that the manager or supervisor is prepared to help and be flexible.

Never believe that a few caring people can't change the world. For, indeed, that's all who ever have. – Margaret Mead

- **Irresponsible** - Lacking a sense of responsibility for self and others. Once we are given a task to complete, do we complete it or do we leave it until the very last minute and then make a hash of it? We need to be responsible for the tasks we face. When we are irresponsible we fail ourselves, our family, our team, and our company. This sort of failure simply makes us stand out as a failure to make the grade in the company.

Let us all take more responsibility, not only for ourselves and our families, but for our communities and our country. – Bill Clinton

- **Dishonest** - Disposed to lying and cheating; deceitful. Dishonesty will always show in attitudes and actions. It is catching in that one dishonest person will encourage others to be dishonest. A company cannot survive if there is a culture of dishonesty among the workers.

In order to be profoundly dishonest, a person must have one of two qualities – either he is unscrupulously ambitious or he is unswervingly egocentric. – Maya Angelou

- **Enigma** – One who is puzzling or ambiguous; playing both sides at once. Remember that sometimes someone will not understand us. It does not matter how clear we try to be or how open. What matters is that something we do will make them think that they do not understand. That is totally different from the team member who tries to keep everyone off balance by playing one set of team members off against another. It can be helpful when trying to destroy an organization such as in the films "The Three Samurai" or James Bond's "License to Kill," where the main character sets the enemies against one another. This characteristic in a team member is a nightmare for the workers, team leader and directors.

It is decidedly not true that "nice guys finish last," as that highly original American baseball philosopher, Leo Durocher, was alleged to have said. – Alan Greenspan

- **Disempowering** - To deprive of power or influence. Empowering people will always build them up. On the other hand, not giving employees enough power to complete a task that they must do always frustrate and belittles. One team member taking power from another team member will harm and unbalance the team.

Outstanding leaders go out of their way to boost the self-esteem of their personnel. If people believe in themselves, it's amazing what they can accomplish. – Sam Walton

- **Self-righteous** - Piously sure of one's own righteousness; exhibiting pious self-assurance. No one on earth is perfect. Some may think they are approaching perfection, but soon learn that they fall short when heat comes into the situation. Sometimes people will excuse their own behavior and criticize others to make themselves seem righteous. This will always destroy and never builds up.

The company of just and righteous men is better than wealth and a rich estate. – Euripides

- **Impatient** - Unable to tolerate delays; restless; unable to endure opposition. Some people are very patient and you can see similar characteristics passed down from their parents. However, there is a fine line between being patient and being so laid back that the task is never completed. A balance must be struck, and that is difficult in many situations.

A leaf that is destined to grow large is full of grooves and wrinkles at the start. Now if one has no patience and wants it smooth offhand like a willow leaf, there is trouble ahead. – Johann Wolfgang von Goethe

- **Uncommitted** - Not pledged to a specific cause or course of action. Many people are quite happy to receive their paycheck and never commit to anything. Often team leaders will feel that they have to fight these people very hard to get a commitment to the task at hand and then get them to complete it.

Unless commitment is made, there are only promises and hopes; but no plans. - Peter Drucker

- **Aggressive** - Inclined to behave in an actively hostile fashion; intense or harsh. This aggression can often be found with impatience in the same person. In some jobs it is essential to show aggression to get the deal or the contract, so no all aggression is bad; however, too much aggression shown towards co-workers can split the team.

Force is all conquering, but its victory short-lived. – Abraham Lincoln

- **Boastful** - To glorify oneself in speech, to talk admiringly about yourself. Sometimes it is hard to see yourself as others see you. It is easier to boast and boost up your own ego. The trouble is that when you come down, you come down hard.

No one but a coward dares to boast he has never known fear. – Ferdinand Foch

- **Critical** - Inclined to judge severely and find fault. It is easy to criticize others, especially when you are a new worker in a company or industry. It is very difficult to see if there are any ruts or bad habits people have gotten into that they need to be helped out of. It also is difficult to correctly evaluate the training needs of some people who may have been in that company or industry a very long time but need to be trained to help them be more useful team members. Someone who continues with a critical spirit will destroy morale and eventually ostracize themselves from other team members.

Sandwich every bit of criticism between two thick layers of praise. – Mary Kay Ash

- **Bad attitude** - A negative state of mind or feeling; bad disposition. Bad attitudes can be displayed in many directions. It may be sexist (male/female) or racially based. The antagonism may stem from an event in a person's life or family history or nation's history. Sometimes these attitudes can be seen as poking fun, at other times it is total animosity. It cannot be allowed to grow in a team, as it eventually will destroy the team.

Your mental attitude is something you can control outright and you must use self-discipline until you create a positive mental attitude...your mental attitude attracts to you everything that makes you what you are. – Napoleon Hill

- **No empathy** - Not showing empathy or caring about another's state of feeling or mind. "We are not alone" may sound like something from a science fiction drama, but too many people see themselves as loners and not dependent on anyone else. It does not work. When we work together we are always interconnected and our best work can

93

only be done when everyone on the team is playing to their strengths and minimizing their weakness.

We cannot live only for ourselves. A thousand fibers connect us with our fellow men and among those fibers as sympathetic threads, our actions run as causes, and they come back to us as effects. – Herman Melville

- **Imbalanced** - A lack of balance; thrown out of equilibrium. All of us face situations from time to time that throw us out of our normal balance. That is the way life works. However, when we seem to be continually out of balance we affect the teams we work in and the management of those teams.

There is an immutable conflict at work in life and in business, a constant battle between peace and chaos. Neither can be mastered, but both can be influenced. How you go about it is the key to success. – Philip Knight

Negative leaders hold power because people in the group willingly choose to follow them. Why would anyone choose to follow a negative leader? Because of some basic human needs we all have, which can meet through group think, group identity, and group pride.

Group Think

Group think is a distorted, unhealthy way of sharing information with group members. Group think is peer pressure. Members believe they must agree with whatever are the leader's fixed ideas for the group to adhere to, either mentally and/or emotionally. It's not unusual for there to be some threat of punishment for those who do not agree with the group. Any member of your group who craves to be a part of group think will continue to let the leader control what they are to think and believe about things. Those attracted to group think do not have the personal integrity (the courage to express what they think and believe regardless of other people's responses) to think for themselves.

World history provides many examples of large crowds who followed negative leaders and joined them in group think. Perhaps you remember Jim Jones and his group in Guyana. At his urging more than 300 of his followers committed mass suicide. Or do you remember the name William Calley? He was one of many involved, but the only one convicted, for his role in the Vietnam War's dreadful My Lai Massacre. Why did Saddam Hussien's group follow him so steadfastly, committing atrocious crimes?

Logically speaking it makes no sense to be a part of group think, but remember, it's more the emotional appeal that this has for group members. There are two more types of emotional appeal – group identity and group pride.

Group Identity

Scott Peck, in his book <u>People of the Lie,</u> talks about how specialized groups can foster group psychological immaturity of its members. He defines these specialized groups as organizations having many layers of people, such as the military or members of a huge corporation. In these groups each member is responsible for only a small part of the whole process that the group will accomplish. As a member of a specialized group, individuals can more easily detach themselves from what the group ultimately will accomplish as a whole. Consider such thinking as "I only okayed the tools to be used to cut down trees in the rain forest" (the unspoken message being "I am not really responsible for cutting them down"). In these large groups it is easier for individuals to pass the moral buck to the next person once they have done their part and feel like they have freed themselves from the group's behaviors. A negative leader could take advantage of this group mentality and often does just that.

Group Pride

Negative leaders can also capitalize on the human desire to be part of something bigger than ourselves. Most groups generate symbols, flags, uniforms, and/or special handshakes that help members connect to other group members in ways that those outside of the group cannot. Group pride works for both positive and negative leaders. For example you can be a member of the Boy Scouts of America, dress in their uniforms, say their pledge, and work together to accomplish good deeds. You can also choose to be a part of a more negative group such as a gang and wear your baseball hat backwards, dress in baggy pants and tattered shirts, carry weapons, and work together to accomplish bad deeds. Sports teams, business teams, educational groups, political groups, and many others all pride themselves on having group pride. Positive group pride can go a long way. Unfortunately, negative group pride also can go an equally long way, if not a bit further.

Another way to instill group pride is to have the group pick out or create an enemy outside of the group who doesn't share the same beliefs. Members can feel a strong connection as they band together to fight this enemy. It's also an easy way for deficiencies in the group to be overlooked while focusing attention on the other group. Hitler ignored all of Germany's homeland problems by focusing on eliminating the Jews.

Stories of group pride have been told time and time again in books, movies, and Broadway show plots. Ever hear of the Sharks and the Jets in West Side Story? How about the Godfather and his enemies? Sports teams have other teams to be the enemy and local high schools all have a big rival school.

How do you know group think is going on, and how do you stop it if you see it? Janis and Mann in their book <u>Decision Making</u> offer symptoms of group think to be on the lookout for. Here are a few examples:

1. **Illusion of vulnerability:** Group members ignore the obvious dangers, take extreme risks, and are overly optimistic.
2. **Collective Rationalization:** Members discredit and explain away warnings contrary to group thinking.
3. **Illusion of Morality:** Members believe their decisions are morally correct, ignoring the ethical consequences of their decisions.
4. **Excessive Stereotyping:** The group creates negative stereotypes of rivals outside the group.
5. **Pressure for Conformity:** Members pressure anyone in the group expressing views contrary to the group's stereotypes or commitments, labeling such opposition as disloyalty.

They also offer some ways to avoid group think, such as:

1. The group should be made aware of the causes and consequences of group think.
2. The leader should give high priority to airing objections and doubts and be accepting of criticism.
3. Outside experts should be included in vital decision-making.
4. Spend time surveying all warning signs from rival groups.
5. Groups should always consider unpopular alternatives, assigning the role of devil's advocate to several strong group members.

Hopefully you now understand something about the dangers of group dynamics that can result in moral and ethical lapses within companies or organizations. Everyone in the company needs to be free to say something is right and true, and something else is wrong. The king who wore nothing was shown up only by the boy who said out loud that he had no clothes on. In the same way moral and ethical constraints on a team or an organization increase when there is freedom to point out the wrongs of planned actions.

10-80-10 Application

Hopefully, you have gained some insights into the 10% of your group that is your negative leaders. Your negative and positive leaders are at the 10% existing at opposite ends of the power struggle. The term "negative leader" may sound like an oxymoron, but in all actuality is a highly accurate term. Negative leaders possess leadership abilities similar to positive leaders; however, they do not exercise their power in the same way or for the same purposes.

Often times, to the detriment of everyone involved, negative leaders are ignored and left to their own devices. Negative leaders, however, have been known to simply and slowly destroy the strongest of groups. Common myths about the negative leaders include: negative leaders are easy to spot, negative leaders do not attract others to them, negative leaders are never successful, and negative leaders are easy to change. Just reviewing these myths ought to alert you to the urgency of identifying who your negative leaders are.

Negative leaders, like positive ones, possess certain qualities and characteristics. Review these lists and commit them to memory. Ask yourself what someone who possessed most of those qualities would be capable of and how they likely would lead anyone who would follow.

Become familiar with the ideas of group think, group identity, and group pride. Each has a lure to followers and will destroy all who choose to follow. Watch for signs of group think. Step in and take immediate action if you see group think going, and set up preventive measures for the future.

And one last time: it cannot be overstressed or overstated that negative leaders, when left to their own devices, will slowly, almost imperceptibly, destroy your group.

Chapter 5: Applying the 10-80-10 Rule

You're now prepared to look at your group and generally determine who's who and whether they tend to be positive leaders, a follower, or negative leaders. Equipped with that information, you can create developmental strategies to facilitate group members' personal and professional growth. Each group has special needs and considerations. The job for the positive leaders is to retain them and teach them how to train the 80% followers. The positive leaders should always be helping shape one of the followers into an effective leader. The followers must develop their own strategies to protect themselves from the influence of negative leaders while learning what it takes to become a leader. The focus on the negative leaders is to turn them around or, if that is not possible, to let them go.

Retaining Your Positive Leaders

Positive leaders are, first and foremost, human beings and need to be treated as such in a holistic manner. This total approach is necessary, as leaders are often carrying the heaviest load in terms of responsibility. Studies have shown that leaders can be up to four times more productive than the rest of the team. That increases the chance they are running on low or empty in their own emotional, spiritual, and physical lives. This is especially true for leaders who are in their mid-life stage, as they are inevitably evaluating their personal and professional lives.

Running low in one or more of these areas is one of the contributing factors to high turnover rates in leadership. Focus on keeping your leaders living a balanced personal and professional life.

Maintaining a Healthy Work/Life Balance

Insist that your positive leaders maintain a healthy work/life balance. Learning to manage personal and professional lives is another way of helping positive leaders learn to take care of themselves. Many of the same elements that benefit their personal life also have carry-over value to their professional life. For instance, if they make time to work out, eat right, get enough sleep, and take advantage of appropriate preventive health screenings, their personal lives will profit. These same profits spill over into their professional life, as they have more energy to do their job, fewer sick days, reduced levels of stress, and an overall happier state of mind from which to work.

Another key element to keeping your positive leaders' work/life balance going is the continual pursuit of personal and professional self-development. Leaders should be encouraged and afforded the opportunity to expand their skills through professional development workshops and other on- and off-site programs. Attending these classes can boost morale, add to their knowledge, increase their awareness of new tools to get the job done with, provide opportunities to network with other professionals, and provide a change in their usual work routine.

Workshops that provide leaders with ways to enhance their relationship skills (remember the EQ) are especially important for leadership growth. Leaders can never learn too much about relating to their colleagues, mentors, teammates, coaches, and others. Again, these skills will spill over into their personal relationships, improving their ability to relate to their family members, their most important group of all.

Another facet of relationship skill-building workshops training are those focused on stress and anger management. In a 2002 poll executives reported working 51 hours a week. The Center for Disease Control and Prevention estimates that 60-70% of all disease and illness is stress-related. In short, leaders are feeling stressed out and overwhelmed. Learning techniques to alleviate and manage their stress is invaluable. Learning to manage their anger is another necessary tool for high-quality relationships off and on the job.

Popular Retaining Possibilities

Professionally, positive leaders need certain things in order to do their job and stay happy. Gallup (in the article "Is Your Company Bleeding Talent?") has identified six areas that are key elements for retaining positive leaders:

1. They need to know what is expected of them. Along with this comes a strong desire to be able to measure their progress toward goals they have been given.

2. A positive leader needs the materials and equipment to get the job done. Making sure leaders have the right tools and resources to get the job done is essential.

3. Leaders need to do what they do best every day. In

short, the demands of the job must match their level of talent and know-how.

4. Leaders need to feel cared about. They need someone to listen to their ideas and concerns. Leaders like to feel appreciated, respected, and recognized for what they do.

5. They need to feel that their followers are committed to the same job they are. Leaders want everyone on the team to be pulling their own weight and contributing all they can.

6. They need opportunities to learn and grow. They should be given the freedom to make mistakes, take risks, create, and grow without the fear of rejection for potential mistakes.

Training Someone to Follow in Their Footsteps

One of the goals of the 10-80-10 Rule is to move members from group to group to strengthen the group and ensure good teamwork. Leaders should always be focused on training someone to take their place, someone who will move out of the 80% followership group and into the positive 10% leadership group. Recall from Chapter 2 that leadership is a learned process, not one reserved for the natural-born or charismatically fortunate. Followers who are interested in learning to lead should be given a mentor whom they can work with and learn from. Many promotions have been awarded to those who follow well.

If positive leaders are not training someone to follow in their footsteps, there's a problem that needs to be addressed. Begin by talking with your positive leaders to find out what they are thinking. Perhaps some of your leaders don't see the value in training others, or they feel too threatened by the idea to want to pursue it. No matter what the case, continually training new leaders is a must for your group to grow and survive. Insist that your positive leaders train new leaders as part of their leadership responsibilities.

Your positive leaders should also be playing an important role in influencing your 80% followers and keeping them away from the negative leaders' influence. It's important that the followers are taught strategies to protect themselves, as opposed to relying on the positive leaders to protect them from the negative leaders. This will result in more self-esteem for the followers and less work for your leaders.

Strategies for Followers to Protect Themselves

Helping followers develop strategies to deal with negative leaders is vital. Many followers are vulnerable to negative influences. They are capable of being easily hurt and are susceptible to criticism or persuasion. If they don't develop ways to stay strong and work their way toward the top 10% of the group, the group will begin to go downhill. An effective strategy followers can learn to use is setting boundaries between them and negative leaders.

Boundaries and People Pleasing

Boundaries are invisible lines that indicate or place

limits on where something stops. The purpose of setting boundaries is to protect ourselves from others. Boundaries are polite ways of telling other people when they are acting in ways that are not acceptable to us. How firmly or weakly we set our boundaries determines how we allow others to treat us. Setting boundaries is a responsible way of taking care of ourselves and protecting ourselves if necessary. Simply put, boundaries make clear separations between us and others. Teach your followers to take responsibility for themselves and make negative leaders take responsibility for themselves.

In order to set boundaries, your followers need to be aware of who they are, what they value, what their needs are, what feelings they have, and how to assertively communicate them. Remember that effective followers do not mindlessly or blindly follow any leader. Should a negative leader assume someone is open to following in this manner and even treats them like it, they must put boundaries in place to stop that kind of treatment. No one has the right to treat your followers this way and they must separate themselves from those that think they do.

Another possible infringement on their boundaries that could be made by negative leaders is expecting followers to do something that violates their conscience. For example, they may try to coerce followers into the group think mode of making fun of someone who is culturally different, or they may even set these different group members up to become their enemies. At this point the follower needs to send a clear message to the negative leader and set the boundary that they will not participate in such behavior. Establishing this boundary alleviates any uncomfortable situations followers could otherwise find themselves in by aligning with the negative leader's behavior.

One reason it is so hard for some people to set boundaries is because deep down it is more important to them to please whoever is leading them. Why would someone want to please their leader? Simple: because they are people-pleaser.

People Pleasing

Trying to please people is the opposite of setting boundaries. Many followers like to please those who are positively and negatively in charge. Followers can sometimes be doing things to please people because they are seeking their approval (whether they are aware of it or not). Trying to please people means your needs are set aside in order to accommodate those of others. Most people-pleaser please out of the fear of rejection.

People-pleaser tend to use a lot of "must" and "should" as they are talking to themselves and others. They believe they must or should do certain things because they need the approval of whoever is placing demands on them. Help people-pleaser develop strategies to keep from feeling like they need to please everyone. Teach them basic tools, such as learning to say "no." Help them see the value of addressing their own needs as well as making efforts to meet other people's needs. Bring it to their attention that negative leaders especially will take advantage of their compulsive desire to please. Keep a sharp eye out for the people-pleaser in your 80%

followers. You don't want them pleasing negative leaders.

Now we have a better picture of the whole of our group. It does not matter if we are responsible for a single team, multiple teams, a complete production site or an entire company. We can now see what the dangers are to the whole team and also to individuals within the team. It would be easy to try and dig out all the negative leaders within our organization, but that would also tear at their followers and may remove good people from the team. So we must deal with negative leaders and try to help them change. Here are the basics for dealing with these negative leaders.

Dealing with Your Negative Leaders

You need to know how to work with your negative leaders. You owe it to team members to have the most psychologically healthy group to participate in. Negative leaders are a fact of life (10% of your group). How they affect your life and your group is up to you. Remember that working with, much less changing, negative behavior is a difficult thing to do. The best you can do is to try and help them.

What's Beneath the Negative Behavior?

The first thing to understand is that negative behavior doesn't just appear out of the blue to be spoken to someone. Beneath the surface of the negative behavior are problems driving it. The key to understanding negative behavior is being able to recognize the seriousness of the underlying issues. You need to generally be able to differentiate between emotional issues that are driving the negative behavior and what are called personality traits that also drive behavior. It is not your job to try and diagnose your negative leaders' underlying issues, but you can learn to note some differences between the two.

Examples of emotional issues would include depression, anxiety, and ADHD. Once a negative leader gets some professional help with their emotional issues, you may see a whole different side to them. If the negative leaders become more willing and open to learning how to manage their emotional issues, they just might be open to moving towards becoming a more positive influence on the group.

Underlying personality traits or disorders that are driving negative behavior can take long-term professional help to make changes. A negative leader who has a personality disorder probably will eventually need to be let go. As hard as that is to do, there is no other way to keep your group afloat and headed toward accomplishing their goals.

One question to ask yourself when working with negative leaders is how coachable/teachable are they? Will they listen and respond to your feedback when you talk with them? As well-respected and well-known motivational speaker Mark Victor Hansen says, "Feedback is the breakfast of champions." Work with the negative leaders to create an action plan full of measurable goals and see how they do. If they refuse to listen and respond to your plans for them, that is a major red flag indicating it's time to give some thought to letting them go.

Ultimate Goal of the 10-80-10 Rule

Remember that the ultimate goal for using the 10-80-10 Rule is to successfully manage the 10% positive leaders, 80% followers, and 10% negative leaders in your group and to work with them with the hopes of having the chance to see some of the members move up the group levels. To accomplish this means spending time observing and then working with each person in each group to help them grow. Moving just one or two members up to the next level would be a real success story. Outstanding leaders could probably move many more members up to the next group.

Ending note

This is not the end. I don't know the details of your team or organization as well as you do. I do not know the people who you view as the negative leaders – you do. The objective of this book has been to help you see your team in a different light. To see the problems of negative leadership. Now you must face the individuals and try to move them forward so they can be more positively behind you and the company's plans and projects. It will not be easy and sometimes you must push them to see if they revert to type and act negatively. You may be surprised that after a while the negative can become a positive for you, your team, and your company.